FAIRACRES PUBLICATIONS 143

FRIENDSHIP IN GOD

The Encounter of Evelyn Underhill and Sorella Maria of Campello

A. M. ALLCHIN

© 2025 SLG Press
First edition 2003
Second revised edition 2025

Fairacres Publications 143

ISBN 978-0-7283-0413-0
Fairacres Publications Series ISSN 0307-1405

SLG Press asserts the right of Arthur MacDonald Allchin to be identified as the author of this work, in accordance with the Copyright Designs and Patents act, 1988.

All rights reserved. No part of this publication may be reproduced, stored in a retrieval system, or transmitted, in any form or by any means, electronic, mechanical, photocopying, recording or otherwise, without the prior permission of the copyright owner.

The publishers have no control over, or responsibility for, any third-party website referred to in this book. All internet addresses given in this book were correct at the time of going to press. The authors and publisher regret any inconvenience caused if addresses have changed or sites have ceased to exist, but can accept no responsibility for any such changes.

Edited and typeset in Palatino Linotype by Julia Craig-McFeely

Biblical quotations are taken from the New Revised Standard Version of the Bible unless otherwise noted.

Cover image: John Ruskin: Under-surface of a dried Spray of Olive (after 1878). Reproduced by kind permission of the Ashmolean Museum, Oxford

SLG Press
Convent of the Incarnation
Fairacres • Oxford
www.slgpress.co.uk

Printed by
Grosvenor Group Ltd, Loughton, Essex

CONTENTS

Introduction		1
I	Discovering Sorella Maria	3
II	Campello: Communion with all the Creatures	15
Appendix to Chapter II: Confraternity of the Spiritual Entente		26
III	Friendship via Prayers and Paper	28
Afterword		47

FRIENDSHIP

IN GOD

Introduction

This small book recounts a series of discoveries. It begins with a first visit made in the autumn of 2000 to the ecumenical monastic community at Bose in Northern Italy.[1] Bose is set in a broad valley with a wonderful view up to the Italian Alps, some seven thousand feet high. In 2003 there were about forty brothers and thirty-five sisters, mostly under the age of fifty and the community now numbers over 100. It is basically an Italian and Roman Catholic community, but since the beginning, there have been members of other nationalities and some who belong to the Churches of the Reformation. The community also has very close relations with the monasteries of the Orthodox East. The life and vigour of this place renew the hopes and expectations of anyone who longs for Christian unity.

At Bose I first discovered the identity of the Sorella Maria to whom Evelyn Underhill refers in her correspondence without ever telling us exactly who she was or where in Italy she lived. There I made a first acquaintance with the story of the community of sisters which she founded in the 1920s, a community of ecumenical vision and aspiration.

The following year I visited the Hermitage at Campello in the Vale of Spoleto, in the Umbrian countryside not far from Assisi. In this second visit I learnt more about Maria herself, and about her English friend and associate Amy Turton, through whom Maria had

---

[1] 'Bose is a community of monks and nuns belonging to different Christian Churches, seeking God in obedience to the Gospel and living in fraternal communion and celibacy. We live in fellowship with men and women and at their service.' https://www.monasterodibose.it/en/ (accessed 19 Feb 2025).

first come into contact with Evelyn Underhill, and with Evelyn's friend Lucy Menzies. I discovered in Maria a gentle but forceful personality, someone of great attractiveness and prophetic insight. Her importance in Italian Catholicism in the middle of the twentieth century is only now coming to be recognized, and she certainly deserves to be better known in the English-speaking world.

In Part III I look at the possible influence of Maria on the development of Evelyn Underhill's life and ministry in the period from 1920 onwards. Evelyn was then becoming widely known as a retreat conductor and spiritual guide, roles which until then few, if any, women had undertaken in any Church. I make the suggestion that some at least of the crucial developments in Evelyn's later life owed much to her deep and growing friendship with Maria, whom she would often refer to as 'my Italian saint'.

The theme of friendship across the years, as well as across the barriers of language and culture, links with the theme of the communion of saints. This resonates with the convictions of Pope John Paul II about the reality of this communion as something already given, despite the continuing differences between the separated Churches. In 2003, the Community of Bose published a substantial and prophetic book, *Il Libro dei Testimoni: Martirologio Ecumenico, (The Book of Witnesses: An Ecumenical Martyrology)*, which gathers in its pages Christians of many ages and many traditions within the one family of Christ, and shows us underlying patterns of unity and reconciliation. This book deserves not only to be translated and adapted for use in the English-speaking world, but to be used and cherished, so that across so many barriers it may help us to build up the unity of God's people both inwardly and outwardly in faith and love.

I
DISCOVERING SORELLA MARIA

Arrival at Bose

Arriving one Saturday afternoon in September 2000 at the ecumenical monastic Community of Bose in northern Italy, I was surprised to find myself talking in a rapid, insistent way about Evelyn Underhill to the monk who was welcoming me. My host was obviously puzzled since, though he spoke excellent English, he had clearly never heard of Evelyn Underhill and was anxious to explain all kinds of practical things like the layout of the community buildings, and to show me where I would be staying. I knew of course why I wanted to enquire about her; it was because I felt there must be someone here who could help me to find out who the Sorella Maria was, the Franciscan Sister whom Evelyn had met in the hills near Assisi in 1925 and who had impressed Evelyn in a way that very few people had done. I had never been able to find anything published about her in English, either in Britain or the United States, apart from the one article which Evelyn Underhill wrote for *The Spectator* in 1929,[2] and the references to her in published letters. But in face of the remarkable and unexpected developments of the community's life at Bose, in relation both to Orthodoxy and the Reformation in the third millennium, my pressing concern about Evelyn's visit to the Hermitage in Umbria seventy-five years ago seemed, on reflection, to be pretty marginal.

Later, after Vespers and the evening meal, I found myself sitting with another of the brothers, the only member of the community

---
[2] 'In Defence of the Faith', *The Spectator*, 13 April 1929, 7.

whom I had met before when he was in Oxford in 1998. He was explaining to me the pattern of the community's worship during the coming week: the Biblical readings which were set and the commemorations which would occur. Monday 4 September would be the feast of the prophet Moses: an Old Testament feast which points to the strong emphasis on the Bible to be found throughout the community's life and worship, and also to the influence of the Eastern Christian tradition where the great saints of the Old Testament are regularly commemorated. 'Monday', he explained, 'is a feast when the regular readings of the morning, midday and evening offices may be replaced by special readings for the day. Tuesday, on the other hand, is a commemoration, and in a commemoration there is no change of the readings in the morning and evening, but at the midday office either a passage written by the person commemorated may be read or a passage about her or him.' 'Tuesday the 5th,' he continued, is the commemoration of Sorella Maria di Campello'.[3] 'So is that', I said, 'the Sister whom Evelyn Underhill met in 1925?' 'Yes,' he replied, in a matter of fact way, 'she is quite an important figure for us, representing a strand in Italian Catholicism with which we feel great affinity. Her teaching and her vision are part of our heritage.' It seemed as if she had taken the initiative and had come to meet me.

Sorella Maria and her Companions

Riccardo began to explain to me something about this woman who in the 1920s had founded a small free community of sisters in a Franciscan hermitage at Campello. For the greater part of her life, she was misunderstood and under ecclesiastical suspicion on account of the wideness, the simplicity and the daring of her views both of religious life and of ecumenical encounter. For about twenty-five years the sisters were not allowed to have Mass at the

---

[3] Sorella Maria (Valeria Pignetti) 1875–1961.

Hermitage, nor to have the Blessed Sacrament reserved there; only from 1950 onwards could Mass be said regularly in their little church. Sorella Maria, however, lived on into the next decade, dying in her eighties in 1961. She saw the coming of Pope John XXIII and of the Second Vatican Council. She died knowing that the things she had lived and struggled for were not rejected by the Church to which she belonged, and which she served with such devotion.

This study is not the place to give any detailed account of Sorella Maria's life and work, or of the nature of her vision; but I soon discovered, by delving into the community's library, that a good deal has been written about Maria in Italian in the last twenty years and that there is also some material on her in German.[4] This is largely on account of her friendship and correspondence with the Lutheran theologian, Friedrich Heiler. I found, for instance, a reference to an article of Heiler's published in 1963, entitled 'A Franciscan Pioneer of the *Una Sancta*, Sorella Maria'. But I could find no reference to anything published in Britain or America apart from Evelyn Underhill's article in *The Spectator*. Among more recent Italian works was a careful, thesis-like study of the relationship between the Hermitage and the ecclesiastical authorities from the 1920s to

---

[4] In German, see Friedrich Heiler, 'Eine Franziskanische Pionerin der Una Sancta, Sorella Maria', in *Neue Wege zur Einen Kirche* (München-Basel, 1963), 40–51. In Italian, see F. Aronica, 'Sorella Maria e il suo Eremo tra opposizione e ostilità. *Storia del rapporto tra l'Eremo e l'autorità ecclessiastica dagli anni '20 agli anni,* 50 (Messina, 1993). The most recent publication [at the time of writing] on Sorella Maria is Roberto Morozzo della Rocca, *Maria dell'Eremo di Campello. Un 'avventura spirituale nell'Italia del Novecento* (Guerini e Associati, 2000). This is an excellent introduction to her life and works. [since the first edition of this book there is also Marzia Cescia, *Maria di Campello: In sconfinata compagnia* (Edizioni Messaggero Padova, 2020). In the United States, Sorella Maria was known in the 1930s through the writings of Vida Scudder. A professor at Wellesley College, translator of the Letters of St Catherine of Siena and a writer on spiritual and social questions, Vida Scudder was much impressed by her contact with Maria and writes about her in a number of places.

1950, entitled *Sorella Maria and her Hermitage, Opposition and Hostility*.[5] This book contains a good deal of official and personal correspondence, (including a long letter from Maria to Pius XII written in 1942, and another to John XXIII in February 1959), and gives also a brief account of those characteristics of her community which most troubled the ecclesiastical authorities at the time.

First, there was her resolute determination to open the hospitality of the Hermitage to all who might wish to come, whatever their religious, social or political convictions. Universality of welcome was for Sorella Maria one of the distinctive marks of the Franciscan calling which she believed was hers. Secondly, there was her equally firm resolve not to allow the community to be enclosed 'in an institution with fixed rules and ecclesiastical approbation'. It was not that the life of the sisters would be lax or irregular; it was to be an intense life of common prayer and shared work, of silence and contemplation, of faith working by love; but it was not to be burdened with the prescriptions of canon law. Both these things troubled the authorities, and there was worse to come. Most serious was her long-standing personal friendship with the most notorious Catholic Modernist of the time, Ernesto Buonaiuti (1881–1946), a man who himself deserves further study. He was not only excommunicated in 1921, but was declared *vitandus* in 1926, one whose company was to be avoided by the faithful. Then there was her constant reliance on the support and friendship of an English resident in Siena, Amy Turton (1858–1942). This is the Miss Turton to whom Evelyn refers in her letters about her visit to the Hermitage. Miss Turton was an Anglican.

It was through Amy Turton that Evelyn Underhill was first brought in touch with Maria as early as 1919 or 1920. All three were involved at that time in the formation of an almost secret network of friends called the 'Spiritual Entente', a group joined together in

---

[5] Aronica D. Ferdinando, *Sorella Maria e il suo eremo tra opposizione e ostilità. Storia del rapporto tra l'Eremo e l'autorità ecclesiastica dagli anni '20 agli anni '50* (Editirice Coop. S. Tom. Messina, 1993).

prayer for unity, 'with no meetings, no rules'; its members were to be seekers after the presence of God, to be capable of prayer, and firmly loyal to their own Church. For Evelyn Underhill it was an extremely important contact at a decisive point in her life. Dana Greene, in a major study of her life and work, suggests that it was one of the principal factors which led Evelyn back into active communicant membership of the Church in which she had been baptized and confirmed. In the story of Sorella Maria, Amy Turton plays a quiet supporting role. But the more one looks the clearer the significance of that supporting role becomes. In the first place Amy Turton was almost twenty years older than Maria and her companions. Maria, like Evelyn Underhill, was born in 1875; Amy Turton was born in 1858. At the time when the community was beginning she was already in her sixties, hence her two nicknames: first and more often *Nonna Amata*, Beloved Granny, or sometimes *Nonna Speranza*, Granny Hope.

Amy Turton was an experienced woman and apparently wealthy enough to be able to give considerable help to the community in acquiring the property where they lived and repairing the buildings of the Hermitage. She was both a friend and a benefactor. A devout and thoughtful Anglo-Catholic, she had lived long in Italy and had for some time worked with Italian Catholics. While remaining firm in her Anglican conviction, she was fully ecumenical in her activities. Maria was evidently completely happy with this position and there never seems to have been a question about it between them; on the contrary they complemented and supported one another.

International and Ecumenical Friendships

But if Amy Turton was a devout and practising Anglo-Catholic, she was certainly in no sense a rigid or narrow-minded one. From her first meeting with Maria in 1919 she saw in the younger woman a spiritual vision and a power of leadership which impressed her greatly. She became herself an admirer and follower of Maria, attracted by the radical newness of her vision of Franciscan life. But she was not only a follower, she was also prepared at times to take the lead. It was through Amy Turton that the community acquired many contacts in the English-speaking world, including Evelyn Underhill. Amy and Maria decided between them that Amy would keep the apartment where she lived in Siena; she had commitments there which she could not abandon. It was planned that she should spend half the year at Siena and half the year at the Hermitage with the community, thus retaining a measure of independence whilst still being clearly identified with the community itself.

Amy also had friends in India. In 1922 she had translated part of a small book on Sadhu Sundar Singh into Italian. Maria was captivated, and suddenly 'she felt she loved him as a brother'. They began to correspond with him and translated B. H. Streeter's fuller study of the Sadhu. This contact with Sadhu Sundar Singh may be seen as the prologue to a longer and more substantial Indian friendship and correspondence, that with Mahatma Gandhi. Here again the intervention of Amy Turton was of vital significance. She already had contacts with the circle around Gandhi through her friendship with Verrier Elwin, and it was through her that Maria first wrote to Gandhi on 24 August 1928: 'Brother Gandhi, here is a little sister for you from now on. I belong to Christ and I am an Italian.' Maria goes on to speak of herself and her sisters, of their life of prayer and silence and poverty, of their longing for peace and reconciliation, and of their love and admiration for him and his work. Gandhi's reply came less than a month later. It is a brief letter of thanks and greeting saying that he has sent her letter on to C. F. Andrews.

This was to become more than simply a correspondence between Gandhi and Maria. On Maria's side her sisters, and in particular *Nonna Amata*, were involved; on Gandhi's side some of his most immediate associates were also concerned—Mahadev Desai and Mirabehn and his two closest Anglican friends, C. F. Andrews and Verrier Elwin. The high point of this relationship came on 13 December 1931, when Gandhi was in Rome; he, Mirabehn and Shamrao met Maria, Amata and Sorella Immacolatella in the Villa Morris. It was for both parties a meeting which was not to be forgotten. Henceforth 13 December was kept as a day of commemoration in the Hermitage. A relationship of love and prayer was built up; for a time, when Gandhi was in prison, both groups agreed to sing together 'Lead Kindly Light' (in Gujarati and Italian) at sunset on Fridays in order to be linked at a specific time in prayer.

The correspondence between Maria and Gandhi is an aspect of her life which has attracted some attention in Italy in recent years.[6] Her letters give many indications of how deeply her prayer and thought and love were drawn towards him. In a letter of 14 September 1935 she writes:

> Yesterday, Friday, thinking of you, of dear India and singing with the sisters 'Lead kindly Light', I asked myself, 'Am I faithful to my friendship with Bapu? I don't write to him: I do nothing for him.' And my heart replied, 'Yes, you are faithful, because you simply live, suffer, work, rejoice and love for clarity and for clarification, for non-violence and mature gentleness, for the humble but passionate search for truth.' So, my great friend, I offer you my faithful offering of love, veneration and gratitude.

It is a passage which tells us much about the way in which Maria lived her life as a prayer with and for others, with and for the whole creation. It also tells us much of the width and inclusiveness of her vision, altogether transcending conventional lines of demarcation, religious, political and national.

Often Maria would write to Gandhi simply with news of the community's life. Thus, in April 1933 she told him:

> Amata, who has been united to us for so many years by the sacred bond of friendship, was received on 25th March as a novice in our

---

[6] See Joseph Patmury, *Gandhiji and Sister Maria* (Asian Trading Corporation, 1998) for the following quotations from Maria's letters to Gandhi.

community. The religious sincerity of the seventy-five year old novice is indeed moving!

Again in 1935, she writes recalling the time when the three of them had met Gandhi and his companions in Rome in 1931, and again she speaks of Amata. 'Her presence with us is a continual blessing. How she prays; how she is "less", how she loves you!'

When the war came, Amy Turton was in her eighties, and it is clear that she decided to stay in Italy with her Italian friends and sisters of so many years. Maria not only wrote about her to Gandhi, she also mentioned her in a long letter to Pope Pius XII, written in June 1942. She writes with respect, but also with great simplicity and frankness in setting out before him her own situation and that of the community. She writes about *Nonna Amata*; one feels that anyone less open than Maria would simply have passed over in silence the existence of the old lady, but being Maria she is determined to be honest. She describes her as a *donna santa di nobile famiglia*:

> She is Anglican by birth and she has the most Catholic spirit that I know. By now failing in powers, she still supports us by the example of her unconquered faith and her angelic recollection.[7]

Maria goes on to say that some priests had hoped for her conversion, and had encouraged her to think the matter over.

> She has always replied, 'I venerate the Roman Church, and so I am united with all Catholics and with all sincere Christians. But I desire to remain faithful to the Church of my birth and my family.'

The letter ends with a moving plea that the community might have permission for Mass to be celebrated at the Hermitage, and that the

---

[7] Copies of Maria's letters to Pius XII were kept in the archive at Campello, as are the letters she received, including those from Evelyn Underhill which are not included in the publication of Underhill's correspondence: Charles Williams, *The Letters of Evelyn Underhill* (Longmans, Green and Company, 1943, repr. Darton, Longman and Todd, 1991). The letters are uncatalogued and are only referred to here by date.

disapproval of the diocesan authorities and of the Archbishop of Spoleto should be withdrawn.

Here, in the middle of World War II, an unknown Italian woman in her late sixties is writing to the Pope about a long-standing spiritual friendship between herself and an English companion who was also an Anglican. What could be more fragile in worldly terms than the relationship between these two elderly, unknown women? Yet surely, looking back now and seeing both figures, the Catholic and the Anglican, in the context of those they knew and loved, we have one of the great ecumenical friendships of the twentieth century. Much has been written about Lord Halifax and the Abbé Portal and the Louvain conversations; something at least has been written about Evelyn Underhill and Friedrich von Hügel; here in Amy Turton and Sorella Maria, is another sign of the power of divine grace to break through the barriers created by human fear and ignorance and violence.

Present Recognition

Equally striking is the fact that both Sorella Maria and Evelyn Underhill, whom Amy Turton brought together, should now be publicly recognized and commemorated in the worship of the Church; Maria in the calendar of Bose, Evelyn in the calendars of the Church of England and the Episcopal Church of the USA. Neither Evelyn nor Maria had received much attention from the Church in their own lifetimes; both have been recognized since their death as figures of prophetic significance.

Certainly at the level of material daily life, there was much that separated Evelyn Underhill from Sorella Maria. Evelyn in her comfortable Kensington home, an almost compulsive writer, with her pioneering ministry as a retreat conductor and a spiritual director in the last fifteen years of her life; Maria and her small, precarious community of sisters, inhabiting an historic place of Benedictine and Franciscan prayer, of intense natural beauty but without drinking water and electricity, and living deprived of the Eucharist for many years and under the disapproval of the local church. There was indeed much in their circumstances that separated them; yet when they met, they immediately saw in one another the reality of a commitment to the one Christ and the gift of the one Spirit. They had a profound sense of the unity of all Christians in Christ as something already given. From that starting-point they looked out into the whole of humanity. Both were strongly attracted towards India; Evelyn in the earlier years of her collaboration with Rabindranath Tagore, Maria in her long and faithful correspondence with Gandhi. Both in different ways were deeply affected by the message and the person of St Francis, above all in their sense of the sacramental quality of human relationships and the whole of creation. For those who have long known and valued the vision and teaching of Evelyn Underhill, now to discover something more of the life of her Italian friend is to find Evelyn's own position again and to see it in a new light. Charles Williams in his edition of the letters,[8] and Margaret Cropper in the first biography of Evelyn Underhill,[9] both underline the importance of this friendship. Although Evelyn and Maria only met once in the autumn of 1925, as Margaret Cropper writes,

> Like the single meeting between George Herbert and Nicholas Ferrar, [this meeting] led to a spiritual intimacy. Years afterwards I remember Evelyn telling me how she could write about her spiritual troubles to Maria and how the short and telling replies comforted and sustained her.[10]

The quality of those replies can be guessed at from the word which Maria gave to Evelyn on the occasion of their one and only meeting:

> As we sat in the woods I asked her [Maria] to tell me something of her conception of the spiritual life. She replied, in words startlingly

---

[8] References below refer to the 1991 edition.
[9] Margaret Cropper, *Life of Evelyn Underhill* (Harper, 1958, repr. SkyLight Paths, 2002).
[10] Cropper, *Life*, 133.

at variance with the peaceful surroundings, '*In tormento e travaglio servire i fratelli*' (in torment and travail to serve the brethren).[11]

In Dana Greene's study of Evelyn's unpublished, private notebooks[12]—the one work which gives us a direct insight into the writer's own inner development—we can see how closely Maria was associated with Evelyn in prayer at decisive moments in her life, as for instance in the early 1920s when her public ministry of retreat conducting and lecturing was just beginning. It seems clear that five years before they met the two women were already intimately united in their prayer for one another and for the unity of all humanity and all creation in God.

An Ecumenical Inheritance

As the days passed, and as I had time to look further into the writings about Maria, particularly the collection of letters and memories put together by Amy Turton in 1929, I began to appreciate more strongly the relevance of my being at Bose to my original thoughts about Evelyn and her friendship with Sorella Maria. In recent years the vision of Sorella Maria, which in her own lifetime was hidden in the hills of Umbria, has become more widely known in Italy and has flowered in ways she would hardly have foreseen. Certainly at Bose she is a quiet, humble presence, not only through the annual commemoration on 5th September, but in the use of her words and thoughts in the regular prayer of the community. Compline is said by the community together only on Sunday evening. It is a service which has a particularly homely feel to it. For the other offices the brothers and sisters put on white monastic albs; for this office they come in their ordinary everyday clothes. It begins with a six verse hymn, sung to a haunting Italian folk tune. The words are written

---

[11] Cropper, *Life*, 148.
[12] Dana Greene, *Fragments from an Inner Life: The Notebooks of Evelyn Underhill* (Wipf & Stock, 2011).

by Sorella Maria and they have their origin in the practice, during the summer months at Campello, of the whole community with their guests gathering for an hour before sunset under the trees to keep a time of silence together, and to pray, sing and read passages from Scripture and other religious writings. Maria wrote to Gandhi,

> It is a time of great gentleness and peace, in which we feel in communion with all our dear ones far away and with all creation.

Something of the quality of this time is expressed in Maria's hymn with its Franciscan joy in the beauty of nature, and in the thrice repeated refrain 'Peace, peace, peace' in which we surely hear an echo of the Indian invocation 'Shantih, shantih, shantih'.

> We come to greet the dying day
> And to ask forgiveness of the Creator.
> And peace, peace, peace we leave to you,
> All health and peace to you we love so much.
> And peace, peace, peace to those who are distressed,
> To the poor, the wanderers and the sick.
>
> And peace to mother earth and peace to the sea
> And peace to those who must travel far away.
> And peace, peace, peace to our departed,
> May heaven grant them salvation and light.
> And now we stay with our thoughts fixed
> In God, who in his mystery makes us his own.[13]

---

[13] From the Campello archives; my translation.

11
CAMPELLO: COMMUNION WITH ALL THE CREATURES

Visiting Campello

My first visit to Campello was with my friend Christopher Armstrong in April 2001.[14] Although there were then only three full members of the community at Campello, not only the spirit but the actual pattern and rhythm of daily life, as it evolved in the time of Sorella Maria—the alternations of silence and speech, of prayer and work, of solitude and sharing—were maintained with joy as well as with devotion.

The Eremo itself is in a most beautiful and inspiring position, high up on the hillside above the Wells of Clitumnus, with wide views across the Vale of Spoleto, to the mountain peaks on the far side. I emphasize the beauty of the place because during the days we spent there the weather was not particularly attractive. It was the end of April, but there was a strong, cold, north wind which brought snow to the neighbouring mountain tops and when the wind dropped the clouds gathered and we had days of light but continuous rain. How beautiful the place would be in spring sunshine!

The community itself occupies a Franciscan hermitage from the fourteenth century, dedicated to St Antony of Egypt, a simple and picturesque group of conventual buildings. Hermits from Egypt and Syria are reputed to have come here in the earliest centuries of the

[14] Former vicar of Aberderon and author of the biography, *Evelyn Underhill* (Mowbray, 1975).

Church's life, and later, Benedictine monks found it a place of retreat. Its situation so high up on the hillside has in the past made it difficult of access, and when Sorella Maria and her companions first came there in 1926 there was a great deal to be done to restore and improve the buildings themselves. Now they are maintained with great care, and repair work after the earthquake in 1997 is going ahead steadily.

In the brief time that I spent at the Hermitage I was generously given access to large parts of the community archive. There was much more than I could cope with in the time available, especially since most of the material was in Italian, but there was enough to show clearly that Sorella Maria was far ahead of her time. The contribution of Amy Turton was also significant, particularly for the international and ecumenical outreach of the place. When Maria and Amy first met in 1921, both already had a vision of what they wanted to do. Maria's vision was of a free community of sisters who would renew in the twentieth century the original Franciscan vision of a life of poverty, simplicity, openness and hospitality to all. Amy for her part had long dreamed of forming an association to pray and work for Christian unity. This she had already called in her mind 'The Spiritual Entente' *(L'Intesa Spirituale)*, the name by which it has been known since then.

Dreams of Unity

Maria and Amy had very different backgrounds and very different temperaments. Perhaps their greatest difference was that, as Amy herself put it later, 'Maria lived her vision, I dreamed mine'. Amy may have been less than fair to herself in summing up the situation like this, but it is clear that the idea of an association of people of different Christian traditions, dedicated to pray for the increase of love, understanding and unity between those traditions, had been with her since at least 1887, and she had hesitated long over how to realize it. She speaks of 'a waking dream', and the final text in which she describes it is called 'A Modern Parable'. There is a great mountain on which there are many ways up and where a variety of people are travelling. The different ways are separated from one another by walls which at the lower stages are high and very solid but which become lower and less clearly divided nearer the top, so that at the end all the climbers are united together in their common approach to the summit. The way up however is not without its complications and difficulties. One of the interesting features of the vision is that the function of the dividing walls is not only negative. At least at the early stages of the ascent, they provide guidance and direction. Only as the ascent proceeds do the climbers begin to feel that the walls are narrowing and hinder them.

And then there are places where the walls are broken down and allow movement from one way of ascent to another. But these places too are a cause both of difficulty and encouragement. Sometimes those who have passed from one way to another are themselves perplexed about the path, sometimes those who are following them are disturbed and troubled at their change. A voice declares,

> Change of road is not God's will for those who know him, since every road alike leads up to him. Each soul has to proceed forward from where God placed him in order to reach the altitude where divisions cease and truth is known as one and omnipresent.[15]

Amy Turton was living in Italy, involved in the training and education of nurses. In this pioneering work she had been much encouraged by Florence Nightingale whom she met in 1896, and whose achievement she was trying to make better known in Italy. All her life Amy remained a whole-hearted Anglican, but her daily experience told her that the love of Christ is to be found active and at work in people of very different denominations—Roman Catholic, Anglican and Waldensian—to mention only those whom

---

[15] Università di Urbino, Centro studi per la storia del modernismo, *Fonti e documenti*, vols. 16–17 (Istituto di storia dell'Università di Urbino, 1990), 230.

she was constantly meeting. She seems to have settled in Siena where she became devoted to Saint Catherine. Through her friendship with an older English resident, Francesca Alexander, a collector of Italian folk songs and tales who was a friend and disciple of John Ruskin, Amy learned something of the popular faith and piety of the countryside. She came to love those songs,

> which dear Francesca Alexander first taught … in her little top-floor studio where she received mostly her poor friends but where Ruskin also must often have talked with her and heard her sing.[16]

By 1921, Amy, already in her sixties, was long familiar with life in Italy, deeply rooted in Anglo-Catholic faith and prayer, but with a largeness of vision which speaks as much of Florence Nightingale as of the more conventional Anglican models of the time. Maria also had considerable experience of nursing, particularly in World War I. When Amy and Maria met, they saw that they had different visions, but saw too that they could help and complement one another. Maria had the decisiveness, the daring and the courage to put her vision into action. Amy had long meditated hers, but still hesitated as to how to realize it. On one thing they were in total agreement. Amy writes:

> Before knowing each other she and I had held the same belief about hospitality, making no distinction of class, nationality or form of faith, or even those without any acknowledged faith.

It is interesting to see how this simple determination to treat all men and women as equals had far-reaching implications, both for their meetings with people of other faiths like Gandhi and his associates, and for Maria's determination that in the Franciscan family she was founding, there should be complete equality amongst the sisters, something of an innovation for religious congregations of that time. From the very beginning women of social standing with professional qualifications were to live side by side with women from the neighbouring villages, some of whom at the

---

[16] This and the following are from Amy Turton's diaries, kept at Campello.

beginning were illiterate, sharing in a common life of prayer and work inspired by Franciscan ideals of simplicity and poverty.

It was in 1919 that Evelyn Underhill first seems to have heard about the plan for the 'The Spiritual Entente' and she encouraged her new friend Lucy Menzies who was visiting Italy to go to Siena and make contact with Amy Turton. In a spirit of modesty and self-effacement, Amy sometimes tried to make it seem that the idea of the Entente, like that of the community of sisters, had originally come from Maria, but as she herself writes in 1927:

> The Confraternity of the Spiritual Entente, to give it its full name, remains distinct from Maria's mission as I remain distinct from her group, being neither Roman Catholic nor renouncing all possessions. My ability to possess has enabled me to secure an old Franciscan convent through the co-operation of friends of St Francis of various confessions. Maria's help in bringing the CSE into being has almost equalled that of the friend who first discussed it with a priest and patiently modified it as he advised. But it was the Counsellor of my vision [Evelyn Underhill], who really, so to say, brought it to birth in the Spring of 1923.[17]

The basic texts of the CSE (given at the end of this chapter) may now seem dated. They belong to a time when Christians of different churches had hardly begun to meet, let alone to trust and understand one another, and they reflect the situation of the later nineteenth century, rather than that of the twentieth, far less the twenty-first. What we have here, however, is an early realization of a vision of a community of prayer for unity, which Paul Couturier was later to speak of as 'the invisible monastery'.

As we can see from references in her letters, the association was of real and liberating influence to Evelyn Underhill during these years. And although much has changed since then, insistence on respect for other people's convictions, on restraint in the statement of our own views, and on the importance of listening to those from

---

[17] From Amy Turton's papers in the Campello Archive.

whom we differ remains just as necessary today, when the most sharply felt differences are often those which divide members of the same Christian family from one another.

In 1933, in her seventy-fifth year, Amy entered the novitiate at Campello and in 1942 became the first full member of the community to die. She was, however, not the first Anglican to become a full member of the community. That honour goes to an American Episcopalian who first visited Campello in 1928. Thereafter, until the Second World War, Miriam Shaw spent several months each year at Campello, returning regularly to her home near Boston, where, together with a Catholic friend she followed a similar style of life. After the war she resumed her extended visits each year until 1970, when she was prevented by illness and infirmity. She was recognized throughout her life as a full member of the community, and was encouraged to gather around her a little group of fellow Christians who sought to live by the teachings of Sorella Maria. In 1978 she celebrated the fiftieth anniversary of her profession and the community of Campello sent a Sister to the United States to re-affirm their communion with her and with her companions. She lived not far from the Retreat Centre of Adelynrood, north of Boston; where, like Amy Turton, she quietly lived out her vocation as a pioneering Anglican member of a predominantly Roman Catholic community.

We must not limit ourselves

The morning after our arrival at Campello, the first thing that Sister Brigitte suggested to us, knowing that we were interested in the community's origins, was that we should visit the cemetery. Before we set out she explained to us that Sorella Maria had originally wanted the cemetery to be near the convent buildings, but for reasons of civil law this had not been possible. She therefore decided on a site two or three hundred feet higher up, directly above the convent. So we set out in silence and in single file, Sister Brigitte in the lead. To go to the cemetery, she explained, was always to go on a journey of meeting—meeting with the departed who were still so closely with us, and meeting with the Lord in whom we and they were united.

So we went up the path, sometimes taking a zig-zag way, sometimes straight ahead. Some trees along the way had small wooden plaques inscribed with words from the scriptures, from tradition or from the wisdom of the ages. From time to time Sister Brigitte would draw one or other of them to our attention. After a while we passed through the wooden door of the solid enclosure wall around the conventual buildings and came out onto the open hillside. Up we went again, pausing from time to time to look back over the growing vista of the Vale of Spoleto, so much loved by St Francis. The sky was cloudy but there were hints of blue here and there and moving patches of sunlight illumined the scene before us.

Eventually we came to the graveyard itself and were again confronted with a locked gate, a further requirement of civil law. As we went in we passed a large plaque commemorating the members *non-conviventi* who had died and been buried elsewhere. Coming to the graves themselves we found that each grave was marked by a low light enclosure of split branches taking the form of an oblong or oval. The graves are cultivated but only slightly; all is very close to nature, and the shape given to each burial place suggests a ship, perhaps a ship which takes us from this world to the next, or a cradle, perhaps the cradle of our definitive birth into eternal life. At the top stands a tall plain cross, with a steep wooden gable, like those of the mountain valleys of the north, the region from which Maria had originally come. Here too we found her own grave, together with that of some of her first and closest associates: Sister Paula *'L'Unamine'*, a remarkable and scholarly woman, the intellectual of the community's early years. She had been born blind and used a particular form of braille of her own devising. Sister Amata, the beloved 'granny', who had also been known as Granny Hope, is here named simply *The Daughter of Peace*. Each grave is marked by a cross, with the name of the person buried and sometimes a very few facts about them.

We made our way down again in the same atmosphere of stillness and quiet joy, as of an encounter with the mystery of life triumphant over death, which we were celebrating that Easter week. The places on the hillside and the whole arrangement of the burial place itself seemed to bring out simply but vividly the sacramental character of the natural world. The trees, the low bushes, the paths which ascended sometimes abruptly, sometimes more obliquely, all seemed to speak of an understanding and experience of the natural world which respects and discerns its potentially infinite depth. In our visit to the community cemetery, we found that we had been taking part in a small domestic ritual which was altogether without stiffness or artificiality. This same combination of the holy and the homely, of the sacred and the secular, of the serious and the less serious, met us constantly, day by day, in our stay at the Hermitage.

It was therefore not a surprise to discover afterwards, amongst the sayings of the foundress,[18] words such as these:

> How much I believe in the communion of saints. For me it is a certainty which I have from experience not only from faith. I also believe in a mysterious possibility of communion with all creatures. For example those I love: a star, a bird, a flower, a butterfly; they enrich my life and make me gentle like the saints who are my friends.

In a most natural and quite unassuming way, Sorella Maria had discovered and lived the mystery that 'everything that lives is holy'.

> When we enter into communion with that life, our own life is enlarged and deepened. In our friendship with all the creatures, and particularly with those who share the sacred gift of life, our friendship with God is enriched and made new.

---

[18] From Sorella Maria's papers in the Campello Archive, author's translation. These and other texts from Sorella Maria may be found (in Italian) in Marzia Ceschia, *Maria di Campello. In sconfinata compagnia* (Sguardo Dello Spirito, 2020).

In the days we spent at Campello, we constantly felt that the spirit of the Sorella was not far away from us. So again it was no surprise to find these reflections in her writings:

> I believe in relics because through experience it seems to me that things which we use become impregnated by us ... Thus if a fragment of something that a Saint has used comes to us, we must have faith. So, if we keep respectfully something that has belonged to a dear friend, we feel a deeper closeness to them. I have and will always have veneration for these material relics, but one should not stop at the material sense of things; that which remains of the thought of the Saint is undoubtedly more precious and more efficacious than any material remains.

Maria is always at war with anything which narrows our faith and restricts our life and vision:

> Humans always have a tendency to restrict themselves. Christians think that Jesus has redeemed them alone. No, no; all, through the same sufferings, through their faith, even if unconscious, are redeemed by him. We must not limit ourselves to one place; yes, we belong with veneration to the Church of Rome, but we must keep ourselves open to be at one with all.

This desire to include everyone, this confidence in God's all-encompassing grace and mercy relates very specifically to the problem of Christian disunity:

> When we read in the *Sacramentario*, that someone who marries a non-Catholic risks losing their faith, what a fallacious idea that is! Do we Catholics alone have faith? Poor Jesus, he allowed himself, to admire the faith of a pagan (Matt. 8:10) ... If I think about dogmas my little lamp goes out, since I wish to keep it alight I don't think about them! ... How is it possible for people to feel the need for these blinkers!
>
> As for myself, you know one of my innermost wishes is to have in our little community Sisters of different religious confessions, so as to realize amongst ourselves the *Irenikon*, that is union in peace.

Later she comments:

Don't call our dear brothers who belong to different Churches from ours Protestants, that name belongs to those in all churches who stop at the letter and don't go on to the Spirit.

Sorella Maria speaks and writes intuitively, as a poet, not as a systematic or analytical thinker. Her words constantly strike us with the clarity and fire that we find in the words of the Fathers and Mothers of the desert in Egypt, and in the life and sayings of the Brothers and Sisters of St Francis. This renewal in the twentieth century of the original gift of Christian monasticism is celebrated in the brief but remarkable tribute paid to Sorella Maria at the time of her burial on 6 September 1961, by Father Giovanni Vanucci, one of the few clerics amongst her contemporaries who truly understood her:

> There rises in us, those present and those far away, a spontaneous word of gratitude to you, Sorella Maria, for the love wherewith you have loved us and for the love that you have awoken in us, now as we are accompanying your little body to the place of its rest. The light which you have given to the creatures of the Hermitage, near and far, to the Church of Rome and to all the Churches, will never be extinguished. From you we have learnt to love the truth of all creatures and to recognise one sole reality in all. We have learnt from you a love for what is humble and quiet and thus for what is beautiful and hidden, a love for all that suffers and waits, a love for friends and enemies, for those near and for those far away, for those shut out, and those shut in. You have taught us to see in every human being the suffering and hope of the Son of Man. Thank you for having guided us to love pure simplicity, silence, the respect for things and for creatures, gratitude for all being, the Cross and our suffering and that of all.
>
> Thank you, for having shown us that in simple and absolute faithfulness to the Lord Jesus, the faith of East and West, the Church of Rome and all the Churches can meet in the unity of love. Thank you for having given life once more to the essential words of Christianity, that due to the usury of time had become faded, *agape, koinonia, sacrum facere,* peace, brotherhood, mother earth ...
>
> Thank you for bringing back to the old Hermitage the life of the first monks, a life renewed by you with faithfulness to the Spirit

and with newness of forms. None of us think of you as dead, and as we are accompanying you to the grave we are certain that you are in the place of light and communion without end.

The creatures that you have loved and blessed will carry you in their heart always as a gift of peace and faithfulness.[19]

There is certainly much more to be explored in the life and the teaching of Sorella Maria. But perhaps the greatest of her gifts of vision is her clear understanding that in creation and redemption alike, both in grace and in nature, it is the one work and wisdom of the one Lord of all that is to be found. Evelyn at once perceived the identity of Maria's vision with that of her 'old man', Friedrich von Hügel; this is a theme which I examine briefly in the final part.

---

[19] Funeral address preserved in the Campello Archive.

Appendix to Chapter I

(From the Campello Archive, Author's translation)

I

Confraternity of the Spiritual Entente

A brotherhood without vows, rule or special habit, with members of every nationality, class and form of Christian faith.

No names are published. Each Brother or Sister is free to enrol others by giving them the card to sign and keep. Each member is free to leave at any moment if he finds that he is no longer in the spirit of the Confraternity. In this case he will destroy the card, and notify the Brother or Sister who enlisted him.

Object:

To hasten the coming of the Kingdom of God by promoting spiritual union between all believers in Christ.

Means:
1. Prayer. 'Prayer is the only solid link in spiritual things'. Members must be capable of real prayer; striving to be 'true personal servants of our Lord'.
2. Work. Shall be according to the gifts received from God, and undertaken for his Glory. 'The love of God cannot be lazy.' The Spiritual Entente should grow invisibly, from one to another, working like leaven.

II

Promise of the Spiritual Entente

I will seek, with the aid of Our Lord, to meet every Christian as a brother. I will strive, by opening my own soul to God's grace, to find him in the soul of every Christian, and to treat with reverence his form of worship.

I will by God's grace, when with Christian brethren of different confessions from my own, refrain from criticism or expressions of disbelief in any doctrine that is true to them; and I will seek to diffuse this spirit around me.

To my brother who doubts the form of faith in which he was born, I will suggest the seeking of counsel from persons who are really spiritual and illuminated; for God has shown me that he is in every soul which verily loves him, believes in him and serves him; and that his flock is being led by different roads to the one fold where there is 'One only flock, one only shepherd—Jesus Christ'.

Signature:
Date:

Prayer of the Confraternity: The Prayer of St Catherine

Come Holy Spirit into my heart; draw it to Thee by Thine ineffable love, and bestow on me charity with fear. Keep me, O Christ, from every evil thought. Warm me and illuminate me by Thy most sweet love, that every pain may seem light to me. My Heavenly Father, my sweet Lord, I pray Thee help me in my every service in all

III
Friendship via Prayers and Paper

Meeting at Campello

In the two previous parts I have written about the discovery of Sorella Maria of Campello. I want now to see a little more of the relationship between Sorella Maria and Evelyn Underhill, in particular through making use of a few of Evelyn's unpublished letters to Maria which are kept at Campello.

Evelyn Underhill died on 15 June 1941 in her sixty-sixth year. I first knew of her name some five or six years later when Father Robert Llewellyn, who came to be our school chaplain at Westminster for one year, introduced me to the selection of her letters, which had been published in 1943 by Charles Williams. From the outset it fascinated and puzzled me. On the one hand Evelyn so evidently belonged to the world I knew, her photograph opposite the title page of the book might almost have been one of my own aunts; but on the other hand the book opened a door onto a whole new world of life and thought and experience, a world full of people with names like Ruysbroeck, Jacopone da Todi, de Caussade and von Hügel. How did these worlds fit together?

One of the intriguing features of the book was to be found in Evelyn's insistent references to 'my Italian saint', a person with whom she seemed to be in fairly regular contact, but about whose actual whereabouts and identity she was strangely reticent. She was clearly much impressed by this person, but who was she?

Already in this account we have been getting to know Maria, to see something of her combination of firmness and sensitivity.

Here is Evelyn's own description of her, from a letter written in September 1925, on the occasion of her first and only visit to Maria's community.[20] It is addressed to an invalid friend living in north Kensington, who had herself already been in touch with Maria:

> ... Maria is all we felt. I got to the little station at five yesterday evening: it was just getting lovely after the heat; and then drove in the little village cab through the most beautiful country, olive woods and vineyards to the hills beyond; and just as we neared the Rifugio Miss Turton and Maria met me and I walked up with them. Maria and the Sisters have white cotton frocks, grey linen aprons, the cord of St Francis and sandals on their bare feet. In chapel they have white aprons and white veils. Maria has the most beautiful expression, strong and humble, and a gentle voice. I got quite a good deal of talk with her; it was wonderful to find how exactly she and my Old Man [von Hügel] agree, in spite of great differences in mind and language, in all the deep things of the spiritual life. We talked a lot about X ... Maria said her soul was 'always very present to her'. I told her X had been asking me to increase the time she might give to prayer and asked her whether she would give her more. She said at once, with surprising decision and authority, that instead of giving her more time, *she* would rather make her reduce the time—*but* X was 'an immoderate soul' though very good and humble, and had to 'learn the way of simplicity' and make her whole life a prayer instead of wanting long special times for it. I said I felt less and less confident to direct her and was afraid of holding her back—but Maria said my holding her back was 'not only useful but necessary to X'. It was just the same bracing treatment that I have long been used to! Though coming with such gentleness.
>
> They have a little shrine of Our Lady on the staircase and yesterday evening we all said the Rosary there. Maria used your rosary as I felt sure you would like that and Miss Turton mine and I hers. There was an Italian priest there too, who came to meet me

---

[20] At the time of Evelyn's visit in 1925, the Sisters were living in a house called the 'Rifugio', not far from the 'Eremo', into which they moved in 1926, the seventh centenary of the death of St Francis.

> because he knew my Old Man and years ago had been helped by him and owed him everything, so wanted to hear his latest news, and this morning he said Mass in their tiny chapel, and Maria served and she and the Little Sisters made their communions ... They put in 'our father St Francis', in the confession, etc., and have special Franciscan collects, and the Mass was for the unity of the whole Church.[21]

There is much that might be said about this passage from the letter, but I note here just one small detail, the exchange of rosaries, a kind of coinherence or perhaps perichoresis in prayer, a simple but moving expression of unity in God's presence.

In another letter, written at the same time, to her Scottish friend Lucy Menzies, Evelyn gives us a vivid glimpse of the end of her stay with the Sisters, when her husband, Hubert Moore, came to collect her.

> Hubert stayed at Assisi while I was at the Rifugio, and picked me up by motor ... A bit astonished, I think, to come in for saying the Angelus on the stairs, and to see me passionately kissed by all the Sorellini on my departure. Maria gave me, at my request, a 'word' to take away with me, and a very ferocious one it was.[22]

This, as we have said, was Evelyn's first and only visit to the Community, but it is clear that she had already been in touch with them for some years. Amy Turton had been one of the first links between Evelyn and Lucy and Maria and the Sisters. In Evelyn's writing, she is always 'Miss Turton': that may in part be due to the respect accorded at that time to a person of an older generation, but remembering how she was always referred to as 'Miss Turton' by the only person I have ever met who knew her personally, I have come to feel that she must have been someone whose gentleness was matched by a certain quality of undeniable authority. Evelyn first visited the community in September 1925. Her friend Lucy

---

[21] Williams, *Letters*, 136–7.
[22] Williams, *Letters*, 159.

Menzies had already stayed there in Lent of the previous year, and Evelyn had written to her on that Palm Sunday:

> Thank you so much for your letters. I have so enjoyed them, especially your account of Maria. I felt sure she was wonderful but you have made me see her quite vividly and now I feel I know her much better than before ... No! I don't know any of them except via prayers and paper; and haven't really done anything particular for the Entente—but it's becoming a curiously strong little organization and the members of its inner circle do seem to be in actual spiritual touch. Your whole account makes me simply long to get out to them and bathe in that atmosphere ...[23]

We can appreciate the strength of the relationships growing between this group of friends, if we look at one or two extracts from Evelyn Underhill's *Green Notebook, 1923–24*. This is a private record of her thoughts and prayers which was only published in 1993, more than fifty years after her death. There, at the very time when Lucy Menzies was visiting Italy, we read:

> March 18, 1924, *Conducting My First Retreat at Pleshey*—had a tremendous circle praying for it. Maria, in Rome, prepared her soul with me. The Baron told me to concentrate on knowing and entering into each individual soul and its needs, even while giving addresses—not just imparting information, but caring for and understanding each angle of approach ... As soon as it began I lost my own prayer utterly—recollection or realization of *any* kind impossible. But was surrounded and supported by *something* which carried me steadily right through it without a quaver or anxiety ...[24]

Here we have a striking instance of the reality of the spiritual contact that can come through prayer. This first retreat at Pleshey was the beginning of Evelyn's work as a retreat conductor, one of the most remarkable and creative of her lines of activity during the twenties and thirties, a development of great significance in the life of the Church of England as a whole, and in the wider Christian

---

[23] Williams, *Letters*, 154.
[24] In Greene, *Fragments*, 59.

world, and it is moving to know that it was being upheld both by her beloved spiritual father, von Hügel, and by this new spiritual friend, Sorella Maria. The hidden and unrecognized communion of Rome with Canterbury was being affirmed and strengthened in ways which at that time would have astounded and dismayed many representatives of the Churches on both sides of the divide. The spread of the retreat movement among lay people as well as clergy in the Anglican world was rooted in this deeply committed ecumenical relationship. The phrase which Evelyn uses about Maria is noteworthy: 'She prepared her soul with me.' Maria stood alongside the English friend she had not yet met, who was about to enter into a way of ministry which had scarcely yet been followed by women, and she identified herself with her wholly.

That the first half of 1924 was a period of rapid growth in Evelyn's inner life is evident from the material in the *Green Notebook*. Only a few weeks later, for instance, she records:

> Going to communion this morning I saw so clearly all the suffering of the world and the self-giving of Christ to heal it, and that communion and the life of union mean and involve taking one's own share in that—not *being* rescued and consoled, but being made into part of his rescuing and ever sacrificed body. And in the sacramental life one accepts that obligation—joins the redeeming spirit-element of the universe.[25]

How central this insight was to Evelyn's prayer at that time we shall see as we go on.

Companions in Prayer and Service

Having become aware of the friendship between Evelyn and Sorella Maria through reading Evelyn's letters, I was naturally eager to see her letters to Maria, which I knew were kept at Campello. I was at first disconcerted, even a little disappointed, by what I found.

---
[25] Greene, *Fragments*, 10.

First there were not so many letters from Evelyn as I had hoped and they were not always dated, though they seem to have been written between about 1928 and 1935. Had there perhaps been earlier and later letters which had gone astray? The letters were mostly shorter than I had expected, sometimes only two sides of an ordinary piece of notepaper, and I discovered they were all in Italian; reading them was going to take longer than I had expected. Then I noticed another thing. Close by, among the Community's Papers, was a much larger bundle of letters written by Lucy Menzies, dating from the early 1920s until after World War II. These were longer, more closely written, more carefully dated; but they too were entirely in Italian. I would have to leave them on one side; they remain there as a treasure for someone else to explore.

As I looked more closely at Evelyn's letters, I began to see them more truly. In the first place, they were primarily working letters, the correspondence of two people for whom prayer and growth in the life of prayer were the principal business of life. All the letters contain requests for prayer, and thanks for prayer: prayer for friends, prayer for people who are ill, prayer for people who are facing difficulties in their own inner life. The question of spiritual guidance constantly recurs. Evelyn's own requests for prayer for herself and others convey both a certain loneliness, and also her sense of living under pressure. She needed someone with whom she could speak in the complete equality of friendship, and also someone on whom she could wholly rely, to whom indeed she could look up. Margaret Cropper notes that

> Maria was a sustaining and loving friend through Evelyn's working life ... She confided to her, I know, much of the pain that came from her own periods of darkness.[26]

(How true this is we shall shortly see). And then Cropper adds, 'Later they saw each other face to face, one of those creative meetings that need not be repeated to bear its own fruit.'

---

[26] Cropper, *Life*, 65.

Among Evelyn's letters we may begin with this one, dated February 1928:[27]

> Thank you for your prayers for the day of retreat for Free Church ministers [*sacerdoti liberi*]; we had more than forty; very worthy and rewarding people, but not much used to silence! Also six priests of the Anglican Church. It was for me a real honour to be their conductor. The meditations were on Adoration, Communion and the Co-operation of the Soul with God.

We see here the ecumenical spirit of Evelyn's activity and we observe that the practice of retreats was at that time very little known in Free Church circles. Evelyn goes on to speak of a further lecture and a time of worship which is to be held in the Cathedral in Bristol, and then of the retreat at Pleshey which will last from March 23 to 26. Only at the end of the letter does she allow herself to expand a little and give some news, and to comment on two writers on whom Maria has apparently asked her opinion:

> As for Tagore and Edward Carpenter, I like the first very much, he is a great poet, the other doesn't please me so much. True he has a sense for life, and is a man with an ideal, but he is not in any way a Christian.

Quite often Evelyn wrote in December, beginning with thanks for the greetings for her birthday on the 6th, and sending greetings in return to the Sisters for the coming Feast of Christmas. A short but substantial example is dated 16 December 1933:

> Thank you so much for your dear letter for my feast. A letter from the Eremo is for me like a message from the little poor man, and brings joy and blessing.
> Without your help I do not know what I should do in my work, because I don't have in myself the purity of soul and the burning charity which is able to carry the activity of God to others.
> I am often in darkness and desolation, sometimes in sorrow, sometimes searching for God, but always seeking to bring

---

[27] This and the following are my own translations from the Campello letters.

consolation, to give a light and a strength which I do not have in myself, to all who ask for it. Therefore, dearest Sister, I beg for the powerful and invisible help of your prayer.

Perhaps the most moving of the letters is the briefest of all. It refers to an incident in Evelyn's life which occurred in 1929, a change which she found it very difficult to accept and live with. One of her closest friends and associates, someone who had at times acted as her secretary, Clara Smith, became a Roman Catholic. Evelyn could only feel this move as a betrayal, a personal loss. From notes which she made during her own retreat in the summer of that year, we know how much she was troubled by it, when she speaks of her

> immoderate longing to retain Clara's full affection and devotedness ... To the question whether I could give up C. entirely, my whole nature answers NO.

But she knows that she has to do it and so she prays for the grace of detachment.

To Maria, Evelyn can only write a letter of total frankness, a letter which is a simple cry of pain. Perhaps the fact that she was writing in Italian made it easier for her to express her feelings so simply and directly, without any of the irony or defensiveness which might have come into a statement in English.

> Now I ask your help because I have altogether lost peace. And the cause is the entry of my dear Clara into the Roman Church — happiness for her, for me the sorrow of an absolute spiritual separation — and I thought her my faithful companion for life. I know well that this cross should be a very salutary suffering; but it is too heavy for my weakness and I am afraid of failing. I ask you to help me. With much love ...

As a matter of fact the break seems to have been less complete than Evelyn had feared, Clara continued as a friend, even if a slightly more distant friend, and in later years was again to be a great help in secretarial matters. But for a moment, it seems, Evelyn's equilibrium was altogether lost.

The vehemence of Evelyn's temperament, and her temptation to become possessive about her friends, were things with which she constantly had to struggle. The vehemence comes out again in a letter of June 1932 to Margaret Cropper. It refers to an incident which took place in a retreat which she had conducted:

> For the first time in a retreat of mine we had the Blessed Sacrament on the altar all the time. I thought, poor fool that I am, how lovely it would be! But as it went on, the awful power of that white eternity seemed more and more overwhelming: it seemed to make noisy nonsense of everything I was trying to say; and I ended feeling like a cross between a monkey and a parrot. Everyone else seemed quite calm and happy, so it was evidently all right for them. But I felt like Angela when she kept saying to her secretary, 'Brother, I blaspheme, I blaspheme'.[28]

In her letter to Maria, Evelyn speaks with even more emphasis describing

> a shattering experience such as I had never known before, an ever clearer view of the profound abyss, the absolute difference between the holy white Eternity and everything I could say, the wretchedness and unworthiness of my words in the face of that silence. In the end I hardly dared to speak; I seemed like a parrot.

Maria seems to have been aware that something strange was happening in this retreat, even before Evelyn had written to tell her, for in another letter to Margaret Cropper, Evelyn writes:

> Last week I got a letter from Sorella Maria, my Italian saint, asking specially how the retreat had gone, as those three days, and especially the last evening, she had suffered so greatly—'far more than usual', and how deeply thankful she would be 'if this suffering had availed for a blessing'.[29]

There is certainly more in these letters than I had time to discover in a brief visit. It would be wrong to give the impression that

---

[28] Cropper, *Life*, 205.
[29] Cropper, *Life*, 204.

they are always reflecting moments of tension and inner struggle. They also contain expressions of simple friendship and news of interesting events. Here is an example from a letter in which Evelyn tells Maria of a meeting with Gandhi in London:

> I spoke with Gandhi for ten minutes. He made an impression of great simplicity, a childlike soul, candid—a little like a bird. The spiritual freedom of the poor is in his heart.

A Message from St Francis

Those who have written with most perception about Evelyn Underhill's early development have recognized the great importance of the journeys to Italy which she made from 1898 onwards nearly every year until the beginning of World War I. She was travelling mostly in company with her mother, sometimes alone. For her, as for many people from northern Europe, to cross the Alps and enter Italy was to discover a new world. Later in life Evelyn was to write,

> Italy, the Holy Land of Europe, the only place left, I suppose, that is really medicinal to the soul ... There is a type of mind which must go there to find itself.[30]

Evelyn's sense of the sacred beauty of that landscape and of the hill-top cities of Umbria and Tuscany is expressed in her writings, where she says: 'In Umbria, clothed with the olive woods where Francis walked ... there is a peace of God eternally established.' She writes of Assisi:

> There is something in the quiet spaces of her streets, in the wonderful way in which she hangs on the slope of the mountain and turns a sheer face to look out over the valley, and the contrast of her pale but warm stones with the prevailing blues and greens of Umbria, which very perfectly expresses the heart of Italy.[31]

---

[30] Cropper, *Life*, 13.
[31] Cropper, *Life*, 20.

In Italy, as a young woman in rebellion against the dry and conventional religion in which she had been brought up, Evelyn became aware of at least three major ways in which she was being led into the inner meaning of the world and beginning to find a way towards its Creator. There was first the sense of the divine beauty present in the world of nature itself and, for her, above all in Umbria. Then there was the sense of that same beauty manifesting itself again in some of the most marvellous creations of human art and architecture, the discovery of the great gifts which a historic tradition of sacred art and meditation is able to embody. Thirdly there was the sense that all this was epitomized in this part of Italy in the person and presence of Francis himself, the little poor man of Assisi in whom joy and grief, suffering and love, were woven together in an altogether unrepeatable way. It need not surprise us how much the meeting with Maria meant to her when in the end it came. In Maria, Evelyn found the life and spirit of Francis present and at work. In her house in Campden Hill Square, she felt herself to be in direct contact with the spirit of St Francis.

In the article about Maria which she published in *The Spectator* in 1929, Evelyn Underhill had written,

> Those who recognize her type will discover without surprise that her delicate courtesy and wide-spreading love conceal a Teresian inflexibility of purpose; a profound sense of the pain and need of the world, and a passionate desire to help it.

Evelyn goes on to remind us of the words which Maria had given her as her own special message, *'In tormento e travaglio servire I fratelli'*. There is joy and there is beauty; there is suffering and there is sacrificial pain. Evelyn records some other words of Maria, in the same article, which bring out the all-inclusive and down-to-earth way in which Maria characteristically recognized the presence of the Divine Wisdom and love in all our relations with the world around us:

> We receive good from the experience which each soul brings to us; from example, from a fraternal warning, from the gaze with which

we follow any creature in reverence of heart, learning to love, venerate, help and pray.

Maria loves to bring together creation in all its God-given aspects, uniting grace with nature in a single penetrating gaze. In seeing these things and keeping them together, Maria was reaffirming some of the deepest of von Hügel's convictions and intuition. For him life in the Spirit must always be both this worldly and other-worldly, natural and spiritual, human and divine:

> The mystic sense flies straight to God and *thinks* it finds all its delight in him alone. But a careful examination always discovers many sensible, institutional and historical contributions to this supposed ineffable experience.[32]

So Evelyn says of von Hügel:

> I cannot but think that this intense consciousness of the close-knit texture of our experiences — of the inter-penetration of the realities within which we live and move — will come to be recognized as von Hügel's ruling intuition and one of the chief contributions made by him to religious thought.

And she continues to quote him:

> We all need one another ... souls, all souls, are deeply interconnected. The Church at its best and deepest is just that — interdependence of all the broken and meek, all the self-oblivion, all the reaching out to God and souls ... nothing is more real than this interconnection. We can suffer for one another — no soul is saved alone and by its own effort.

In one of the greatest of her essays, on the subject, 'St Francis and Franciscan Spirituality',[33] Evelyn speaks of these things in particular by working out the apparently unlikely comparison

---

[32] Williams, *Letters*, 20ff.
[33] 'St Francis and Franciscan Spirituality', Walter Seton Memorial Lecture, 1933, University College, London, 17 Jan 1933, in *Mixed Pasture: Twelve Essays and Addresses* (Methuen, 1933, repr. Wipf & Stock 2015), 147–158.

between the fundamental insights of the twelfth-century Italian friar and the nineteenth-century Anglo-German philosopher and theologian. She writes:

> All readers of the letters of Baron von Hügel will remember the penetrating and unconventional sayings of his director, the saintly Abbé Huvelin: and among them one that strikes us on first reading as a paradox. Huvelin said to the Baron on one occasion, in answer to a question, which is not reported to us, 'Yes, there have been saints, and even great saints, of your type. St Francis of Assisi—I don't mean the Franciscans!—*there* is a Saint wholly cast in the mould of life and movement, light and warmth!'
>
> Those who knew the great scholar saint or knew him from his profound and often difficult teaching, and those who think they know the spirit of St Francis will feel baffled by this judgement. What can there be in common between two so almost comically different human beings?[34]

But Evelyn will not allow us to escape from the question. She has too much respect for St Francis and von Hügel, too much respect for Huvelin himself for that. She insists:

> This is the opinion of a saint, a realist, for whom God was everything, about two other saints, also realists, for whom God was everything; and neither of whom were able to exclude any aspect of his creation from the sphere of their interest and their love.

To the question of what they had in common she replies:

> Both the medieval Friar and the modern scholar were penetrated by a sense of the realness, more the sacredness, of the natural as well as the supernatural order; something which was not to be fled from, but to be loved without possessiveness, with an unlimited and humble tenderness, cleansed of all desire. This is not the outlook of the pious naturalist or the higher pantheist. It is the outlook of the genuine Christian supernaturalist who places nature where it belongs—in the heart of God—and is conscious of his supporting presence through and in the web of life. 'God', said

---

[34] This and the following: 'St Francis and Franciscan Spirituality', 155ff.

von Hügel, 'is a stupendously rich reality; he is the God of nature as well as the God of supernature.' St Francis would have understood and welcomed that. Every movement of his life declares its truth. Hence comes the Franciscan attitude of reverence and delight towards the finite world in which we live; and the humble and friendly love of all those creatures whom von Hügel, in terms St Francis would surely have echoed, called 'Our little relations, the lesser children of God'.

Evelyn continues with a long and searching consideration of the nature of holiness as we see it in St Francis, which brings her in the end to a consideration of two of the great turning points in the life of the saint.

The first point would be that in which it seemed to him that a voice spoke from the crucifix of San Damiano, and demanded his total dedication to its purposes. The second point would be that in which the seraph on La Verna, with its reminiscence of Isaiah's mighty vision of reality, baptised into Christianity and mysteriously united with the suffering of the cross, completed his initiation into the deep secrets of the redemptive order. That overwhelming illumination ruled the last two years of his life ... This was the supreme thing which Francis saw, loved and believed; and that with such intensity, that the love and belief took physical form. Here he found the clue to the meaning of his own life, as a servant and agent of the unseen.

His whole career as I see it is poised on these two strange events. The first drew him out towards the visible world, to help, mend, and serve it. The second made him the mysterious partner of an invisible, rescuing love. Wherever we get him really speaking his mind he is never far from the cross; the underlying tension of life. 'Yes there it is; no need to go further,' said Huvelin. 'Sanctity and suffering are the same thing. You will do no good to others save in suffering and through suffering.' We draw very near the real Francis, though not very near the popular notion of Francis, when we meditate on these words ... The entire growth of Francis was towards the point at which, as that strange phrase in his legend says, 'He was transformed by the kindling of his mind into the image of the crucified', embracing and harmonizing in one movement of self-abandoned love, the splendour of God and the deep suffering of man. That is charity, the outpouring passion of generous love, at its full height, depth, breadth, and width; a passion which is the earnest of eternal life, and reflects back to a metaphysical source. St Francis, says the Fioretti, in a famous passage, offered his followers 'the chalice of life', and those who had the courage to drink it saw in profound contemplation 'the abyss of the infinite divine light'.

Summing up her whole consideration Evelyn Underhill ends with a remarkable claim. What his contemporaries saw in him was, she says:

> a reincarnation as it were of the whole evangelical life in its completeness, its riches and poverty, suffering and beauty, the crib and the cross. He was one in whom, as Jacopone da Todi said plainly, 'Christ was felt to live again', and show in its perfection the right relation of man to God.

There is no mention of Sorella Maria in the pages of this essay, but her presence may be felt silently, discreetly, throughout. As Dana Greene observes, in the period to which this essay belongs, Evelyn's 'early preference for Ruysbroeck seems to have diminished and been replaced by the Italian Franciscans, beginning with St Francis of Assisi.'[35] Of course Dana Greene recognizes that Evelyn continued to value greatly the medieval Flemish and English mystics and the French spiritual writers of the seventeenth to nineteenth centuries. But Angela of Foligno, Jacopone da Todi, and her own contemporary Sorella Maria held a special place. All of them were imbued with the spirit of St Francis. She saw in Francis, as she did in the Orthodox tradition, a sense of the sacred in the natural world and a love and delight in the senses. Francis's creaturely simplicity and awestruck sense of God were also the same characteristics that

---

[35] Greene, *Fragments*, 19.

she found so dominant in her own beloved von Hügel. But the real greatness of Francis she wrote:

> is the same as the greatness of the Christian religion when fully understood. It is one thing to be a believer in Christianity or even a courageous practitioner of its hard demands, another thing to be sensitized to all its mysterious implications: and it is just these mysterious implications which the poetic intuition and intrepid love of Francis seized and expressed in terms of human life.

In the pages of Evelyn's essay we see her at her most impressive, reflecting, in the light both of her profound knowledge of the Christian tradition as a whole and of her own experience of the life of prayer and contemplation, on the truths of the Christian revelation; and in her own characteristic way carrying on a remarkable work of integration, a truly esemplastic activity. She is drawing together the different aspects of the many-sided mystery of God's love, and in doing so she is showing the unifying power of the original Franciscan vision to hold together in one, lines of thought and experience often considered as being distinctly western and Catholic on the one side, or eastern and Orthodox on the other. Bringing us in the end to a distinctly and profoundly hesychastic theme, the contemplation of 'the abyss of the infinite divine light.' We may reflect that it was in these years that she was getting to know Fr Sergius Bulgakov (1871–1944) personally in the context of the annual Conference of the Fellowship of St Alban and St Sergius.

This fuller realization and articulation of the original Franciscan vision in its depth and richness, as well as in its immediate radiance, was, I believe, made possible for Evelyn Underhill by her direct contact with Sorella Maria and with the life and experience of the community which she had founded. This was a life which not only gathered up the past and was open to the future; it was also vividly aware of the needs and possibilities of the present. Not for nothing did Maria enter into correspondence with people whom she believed had some privileged understanding of the way in which the Spirit was guiding the history of her own time, Gandhi, Albert Schweitzer, Friedrich Heiler, Giovanni Vanucci, among others.

But if Maria could be open to all the positive and life-giving work of the Spirit in the world of her own day, she also could not help being aware of the powers of darkness at work in it as well. Here too Evelyn was altogether at one with her. In her meditation on St Francis she speaks of the harmonizing in one movement of self-abandoned love, 'the splendour of God and the deep suffering of man'. These words come from the lecture given in 1933; the year which saw the beginning of an apocalyptic descent into human suffering on the whole continent of Europe, through the rise of Nazism in Germany and Fascism in Italy. Of all this neither Evelyn nor Maria could be unaware. They both of them lived, as Evelyn said of Maria 'with a profound sense of the pain and need of the world, and a passionate desire to help it'. If in the earlier stage of her spiritual journey Evelyn had been greatly attracted to the purely God-ward aspects of religion, to 'the flight of the alone to the Alone', the whole emphasis of the teaching and guidance of von Hügel had been more and more bringing her to a total and committed incarnationalism.

We see this in her later stress on the need for the Church's active presence in the world. In one of the last of her major public lectures she speaks of the need for Christianity

> to spread out far beyond the devotional focus of its life ... It must, in fact have the courage to apply its inherent sacramentation without limit to the whole mixed experience of humanity ...[36]

We see it also in her carefully thought through and tenaciously held pacifist convictions, as the threat of war drew ever nearer; and these were convictions which she did not abandon once the war had come. For while she saw that most of her fellow countrymen, indeed most of her fellow Christians, were quite incapable of taking up that position, she could still write to E. I. Watkin in 1941, 'I've never felt

---

[36] Cropper, *Life*, 214.

an inclination to change my views on the war ... One cannot fight evil by the use of evil.'

We seem to hear again the echo of Maria's word to her friend, *'In tormento e travaglio servire i fratelli'*, in the description which we have from an unknown friend, of the last days of Evelyn's life, in the summer of 1941:

> She had a good bit of pain and she set herself with great fortitude to face the situation ... She sent messages to many people asking prayers for all sufferers, for the union of Christian Churches. She went through a good bit of pain which reached a climax when the distress seemed to be spiritual rather than physical. She was very strange and we thought she was dying. The next moment she became radiantly happy and remained all day in an ecstasy of triumph; from what she said she knew that something had been accomplished and the sufferers would not be disappointed. She was rejoicing in God and Christ in a way which was very different from her normally rather austere devotion, she fell asleep very peacefully.[37]

In its very clumsiness, the description of these last days rings true. There is the vehemence of temperament, the tendency to go to the extremes of spiritual experience, which Evelyn had so long known within herself and had sought to moderate. There is her profound sense of union with all who suffer and with all who long for the unity of the Churches. In the final offering of her own life, there is the evident desire to be united with so many whom she had known and supported, and who had known and supported her. We are reminded too of what she wrote in her private notebook in the summer of 1924:

> Going to Communion this morning I saw so clearly all the suffering of the world and the self-giving of Christ to heal it—and that communion and the life of union mean and involve taking one's own share in that ...[38]

---

[37] Christopher Armstrong, *Evelyn Underhill, 1875–1941: An Introduction to her Life and Writings* (Mowbrays, 1976), 291.
[38] Greene, *Fragments*, 63.

In the midst of a major European war, there could be no direct outward contact between London and Campello; yet who can doubt that there was a union of prayer and love between the two friends who had known each other at such a depth even before they met face to face, and who had so truly supported one another in all the demands of their journey towards God's kingdom.

This meeting of one with the other, is, I believe, of a far wider significance than might at first sight appear. There is a genuinely prophetic quality in the shared vision of these two women, so different from one another yet so evidently at one. Their meeting opens up for us, I believe, the hope and vision of a more courageous prayer and work for unity, certainly within the family of all who confess Christ, but also more widely through the whole human family and through the whole of the world which God has created. For Anglicans in particular, the encounter with Sorella Maria, offers a possibility of re-appropriating central elements of the vision of Evelyn Underhill in a way which is directly relevant to some of the most urgent needs of our own turbulent new century.

AFTERWORD

In the first part of this study, we have seen some of the difficulties which Sorella Maria had in the 1920s and '30s with her diocesan Bishop. For many years the Community of Campello had to live without the full approval and blessing of the local Church. It was undoubtedly this fact which made Evelyn Underhill so reticent about who exactly Maria was and where the Community was situated when she published her article about the Community in *The Spectator* in 1929.

The situation today, not only at Campello but throughout the Christian world, is of course vastly different. We have been thinking here of the reality of the network of prayer which already now binds Christians of different Churches and different traditions together. That is an interchange which is not broken by death. In the Communion of Saints, Francis, Clare, Friedrich von Hügel, Evelyn Underhill, Sorella Maria, Amy Turton continue to pray with us and for us. This sense of the unbroken communion of saints in heaven with those on earth, in which already the wounds of division are being healed, is beautifully expressed by Pope John Paul II in his Encyclical Letter of 1995, *Ut Unum Sint*. These texts are not so well known as they should be, but they are so relevant to the subject of this study, that it seems appropriate to quote a little from them:

> In a theocentric vision, we Christians already have a common Martyrology. This also includes the martyrs of our own century ... and it shows how, at a profound level, God preserves communion among the baptized in the supreme demand of faith, manifested in the sacrifice of life itself. ...

> While for all Christian communities the martyrs are the proof of the power of grace, they are not the only ones to bear witness to that power. Albeit in an invisible way, the communion between our Communities, even if still incomplete, is truly and solidly grounded in the full communion of the Saints—those who, at the end of a life faithful to grace, are in communion with Christ in glory. These Saints come from all the Churches and Ecclesial Communities which gave them entrance into the communion of salvation.
>
> This universal presence of the Saints is in fact a proof of the transcendent power of the Spirit. It is the sign and proof of God's victory over the forces of evil which divide humanity. As the liturgies sing: 'You are glorified in your Saints, but their glory is the crowning of your gifts'. Where there is a sincere desire to follow Christ, the Spirit is often able to pour out his grace in extraordinary ways. The experience of ecumenism has enabled us to understand this better ...[39]

The experience of such ecumenical pioneers as Evelyn and Maria, and the living bonds of love and knowledge which unite them with the friends and companions who sustained and supported them, show us how God's grace is poured out in extraordinary ways, and the transcendent power of the Spirit made known in those who have become true friends of one another in becoming friends of God; those in whom by the Spirit's gift the forces of evil which divide humanity are finally overcome.

---

[39] from Pope John Paul II, Encyclical: *Ut Unum Sint* (25 May 1995), paragraph 84.

SLG PRESS PUBLICATIONS

FP1	*Prayer and the Life of Reconciliation*	Gilbert Shaw (1969)
FP2	*Aloneness not Loneliness*	Mother Mary Clare SLG (1969)
FP4	*Intercession*	Mother Mary Clare SLG (1969)
FP8	*Prayer: Extracts from the Teaching of Father Gilbert Shaw*	Gilbert Shaw (1973)
FP12	*Learning to Pray*	Mother Mary Clare SLG (1970)
FP15	*Death, the Gateway to Life*	Gilbert Shaw (1971, 3/2024)
FP16	*The Victory of the Cross*	Dumitru Stăniloae (1970, 3/2023)
FP26	*The Message of Saint Seraphim*	Irina Gorainov (1974)
FP28	*Julian of Norwich: Four Studies to Commemorate the Sixth Centenary of the Revelations of Divine Love* Sister Benedicta Ward SLG, Sister Eileen Mary SLG, Sister Mary Paul SLG, A. M. Allchin (1973, 3/2022)	
FP43	*The Power of the Name: The Jesus Prayer in Orthodox Spirituality* Kallistos Ware (1974)	
FP46	*Prayer and Contemplation* and *Distractions are for Healing*	
		Robert Llewelyn (1975, 2/2024)
FP48	*The Wisdom of the Desert Fathers*	trans. Sister Benedicta Ward SLG (1975)
FP50	*Letters of Saint Antony the Great*	trans. Derwas Chitty (1975, 2/2021)
FP54	*From Loneliness to Solitude*	Roland Walls (1976)
FP55	*Theology and Spirituality*	Andrew Louth (1976, rev. 1978, 3/2024)
FP61	*Kabir: The Way of Love and Paradox*	Sister Rosemary SLG (1977)
FP62	*Anselm of Canterbury: A Monastic Scholar*	Sister Benedicta Ward SLG (1973, 2/2024)
FP67	*Mary and the Mystery of the Incarnation: An Essay on the Mother of God in the Theology of Karl Barth* Andrew Louth (1977, 2/2024)	
FP68	*Trinity and Incarnation in Anglican Tradition*	A. M. Allchin (1977, 2/2024)
FP70	*Facing Depression*	Gonville ffrench-Beytagh (1978, 2/2020)
FP71	*The Single Person*	Philip Welsh (1979)
FP72	*The Letters of Ammonas, Successor of St Antony* trans. Derwas Chitty, introd. Sebastian Brock (1979, 2/2023)	
FP74	*George Herbert, Priest and Poet*	Kenneth Mason (1980)
FP75	*A Study of Wisdom: Three Tracts by the Author of* The Cloud of Unknowing	
		trans. Clifton Wolters (1980)
FP81	*The Psalms: Prayer Book of the Bible*	Dietrich Bonhoeffer, trans. Sister Isabel SLG (1982, 3/2025)
FP82	*Prayer & Holiness: The Icon of Man Renewed in God*	
		Dumitru Stăniloae (1982, rev. 2/2023)
FP85	*Walter Hilton: Eight Chapters on Perfection & Angels' Song*	
		trans. Rosemary Dorward (1983, rev. 3/2024)
FP88	*Creative Suffering*	Iulia de Beausobre (1989)
FP90	*Bringing Forth Christ: Five Feasts of the Child Jesus by St Bonaventure*	
		trans. Eric Doyle OFM (1984, 3/2024)
FP92	*Gentleness in John of the Cross*	Thomas Kane (1985)
FP94	*Saint Gregory Nazianzen: Selected Poems*	trans. John McGuckin (1986, 2/2024)

FP95 *The World of the Desert Fathers: Stories and Sayings from the Anonymous Series of the Apophthegmata Patrum* trans. Columba Stewart OSB (1986, 2/2020)
FP104 *Growing Old with God* Timothy N. Rudd (1988, 2/2020)
FP106 *Julian Reconsidered* Kenneth Leech, Sister Benedicta Ward SLG (1988/ rev. 2/2024)
FP108 *The Unicorn: Meditations on the Love of God* Harry Galbraith Miller (1989)
FP109 *The Creativity of Diminishment* Sister Anke (1990)
FP110 *Called to be Priests* Hugh Wybrew (1989, updated 2/2024)
FP111 *A Kind of Watershed: An Anglican Lay View of Sacramental Confession*
Christine North (1990, updated 2/2022)
FP116 *Jesus, the Living Lord* Bishop Michael Ramsey (1992)
FP120 *The Monastic Letters of Saint Athanasius the Great*
trans. and introd. Leslie Barnard (1994, 2/2023)
FP122 *The Hidden Joy* Sister Jane SLG, ed. Dorothy Sutherland (1994)
FP124 *Prayer of the Heart: An Approach to Silent Prayer and Prayer in the Night*
Alexander Ryrie (1995, 3/2020)
FP126 *Evelyn Underhill, Anglican Mystic: Two Centenary Essays*
A. M. Allchin, Bishop Michael Ramsey (1977, 3/2025)
FP127 *Apostolate and the Mirrors of Paradox*
Sydney Evans, ed. Andrew Linzey & Brian Horne (1996)
FP128 *The Wisdom of Saint Isaac the Syrian* Sebastian Brock (1997)
FP129 *Saint Thérèse of Lisieux: Her Relevance for Today* Sister Eileen Mary SLG (1997)
FP130 *Expectations: Five Addresses for Those Beginning Ministry* Sister Edmée SLG (1997, 2/2024)
FP131 *Scenes from Animal Life: Fables for the Enneagram Types*
Waltraud Kirschke, trans. Sister Isabel SLG (1998)
FP132 *Praying the Word of God: The Use of Lectio Divina* Charles Dumont OCSO (1999)
FP133 *Love Unknown: Meditations on the Death and Resurrection of Jesus*
John Barton (1999, 2/2024)
FP134 *The Hidden Way of Love: Jean-Pierre de Caussade's Spirituality of Abandonment*
Barry Conaway (1999, 2/2025)
FP135 *Shepherd and Servant: The Spiritual Theology of Saint Dunstan* Douglas Dales (2000)
FP137 *Pilgrimage of the Heart* Sister Benedicta Ward SLG (2001)
FP138 *Mixed Life* Walter Hilton, trans. Rosemary Dorward (2001, enlarged rev. 3/2024)
FP139 *In the Footsteps of the Lord: The Teaching of Abba Isaiah of Scetis*
John Chryssavgis, Luke Penkett (2001, 2/2023)
FP140 *A Great Joy: Reflections on the Meaning of Christmas* Kenneth Mason (2001)
FP141 *Bede and the Psalter* Sister Benedicta Ward SLG (2002, 2/2024)
FP142 *Abhishiktananda: A Memoir of Dom Henri Le Saux* Murray Rogers, David Barton (2003)
FP143 *Friendship in God: The Encounter of Evelyn Underhill & Sorella Maria of Campello*
A. M. Allchin (2003, 2 rev./2025)
FP144 *Christian Imagination in Poetry and Polity: Some Anglican Voices from Temple to Herbert*
Bishop Rowan Williams (2004)
FP145 *The Reflections of Abba Zosimas: Monk of the Palestinian Desert*
trans. and introd. John Chryssavgis (2005, 3/2022)
FP146 *The Gift of Theology: The Trinitarian Vision of Ann Griffiths and Elizabeth of Dijon*
A. M. Allchin (2005)
FP147 *Sacrifice and Spirit* Bishop Michael Ramsey (2005)
FP148 *Saint John Cassian on Prayer* trans. A. M. Casiday (2006, 2/2024)
FP149 *Hymns of Saint Ephrem the Syrian* trans. Mary Hansbury (2006, 2/2024)

FP150	Suffering: Why All this Suffering? What Do I Do about It?	
	Reinhard Körner OCD, trans. Sister Avis Mary SLG (2006)	
FP151	A True Easter: The Synod of Whitby 664 AD	Sister Benedicta Ward SLG (2007, 2/2023)
FP152	Prayer as Self-Offering	Alexander Ryrie (2007)
FP153	From Perfection to the Elixir: How George Herbert Fashioned a Famous Poem	
		Benedick de la Mare (2008, 2/2024)
FP154	The Jesus Prayer: Gospel Soundings	Sister Pauline Margaret CHN (2008)
FP155	Loving God Whatever: Through the Year with Sister Jane	Sister Jane SLG (2006)
FP156	Prayer and Meditation for a Sleepless Night	
		SISTERS OF THE LOVE OF GOD (1993, 3/2024)
FP157	Being There: Caring for the Bereaved	John Porter (2009)
FP158	Learn to Be at Peace: The Practice of Stillness	Andrew Norman (2010)
FP159	From Holy Week to Easter	George Pattison (2010)
FP160	Strength in Weakness: The Scandal of the Cross	John W. Rogerson (2010)
FP161	Augustine Baker: Frontiers of the Spirit	Victor de Waal (2010, 2/2025)
FP162	Out of the Depths	
	Gonville ffrench-Beytagh; epilogue Wendy Robinson (1990, 2/2010)	
FP163	God and Darkness: A Carmelite Perspective	
	Gemma Hinricher OCD, trans. Sister Avis Mary SLG (2010)	
FP164	The Gift of Joy	Curtis Almquist SSJE (2011)
FP165	'I Have Called You Friends': Suggestions for the Spiritual Life Based on	
	the Farewell Discourses of Jesus	Reinhard Körner OCD (2012)
FP166	Leisure	Mother Mary Clare SLG (2012)
FP167	Carmelite Ascent: An Introduction to Saint Teresa and Saint John of the Cross	
		Mother Mary Clare SLG (1973, rev. 2012)
FP168	Ann Griffiths and Her Writings	Llewellyn Cumings (2012)
FP169	The Our Father	Sister Benedicta Ward SLG (2012)
FP171	The Spiritual Wisdom of the Syriac Book of Steps	Robert A. Kitchen (2013)
FP172	The Prayer of Silence	Alexander Ryrie (2012)
FP173	On Tour in Byzantium: Excerpts from The Spiritual Meadow of John Moschus	
		Ralph Martin SSM (2013)
FP174	Monastic Life	Bonnie Thurston (2016)
FP175	Shall All Be Well? Reflections for Holy Week	Graham Ward (2015)
FP176	Solitude and Communion: Papers on the Hermit Life	ed. A. M. Allchin (2015)
FP177	The Prayers of Jacob of Serugh	ed. Mary Hansbury (2015)
FP178	The Monastic Hours of Prayer	Sister Benedicta Ward SLG (2016)
FP179	The Desert of the Heart: Daily Readings with the Desert Fathers	
		trans. Sister Benedicta Ward SLG (2016)
FP180	In Company with Christ: Lent, Palm Sunday, Good Friday & Easter to Pentecost	
		Sister Benedicta Ward SLG (2016)
FP181	Lazarus: Come Out! Reflections on John 11	Bonnie Thurston (2017)
FP182	Unknowing & Astonishment: Meditations on Faith for the Long Haul	
		Christopher Scott (2018)
FP183	Pondering, Praying, Preaching: Romans 8	Bonnie Thurston (2019, 2/2021)
FP184	Shem`on the Graceful: Discourse on the Solitary Life	
		trans. and introd. Mary Hansbury (2020)
FP185	God Under My Roof: Celtic Songs and Blessings	Esther de Waal (2020)
FP186	Journeying with the Jesus Prayer	James F. Wellington (2020)

FP187	Poet of the Word: Re-reading Scripture with Ephraem the Syrian	
		Aelred Partridge OC (2020)
FP188	Identity and Ritual	Alan Griffiths (2021)
FP189	River of the Spirit: The Spirituality of Simon Barrington-Ward	Andy Lord (2021)
FP190	Prayer and the Struggle against Evil	John Barton, Daniel Lloyd, James Ramsay, Alexander Ryrie (2021)
FP191	Dante's Spiritual Journey: A Reading of the Divine Comedy	Tony Dickinson (2021)
FP192	Jesus the Undistorted Image of God	John Townroe (2022)
FP193	Our Deepest Desire: Prayer, Fasting & Almsgiving in the Writings of Saint Augustine of Hippo	Sister Susan SLG (2022)
FP194	Lent with George Herbert	Tony Dickinson (2022)
FP195	Four Ways to the Cross	Tony Dickinson (2022)
FP196	Anselm of Canterbury, Teacher of Prayer	Sister Benedicta Ward SLG (2022)
FP197	With One Heart and Mind: Prayers out of Stillness	Anthony Kemp (2023)
FP198	Sayings of the Urban Fathers & Mothers	James Ashdown (2023)
FP199	Doors	Sister Raphael SLG (2023)
FP200	Monastic Vocation SISTERS OF THE LOVE OF GOD, Bishop Rowan Williams (2021)	
FP201	An Ecology of the Heart: Faith Through the Climate Crisis	Duncan Forbes (2023)
FP202	'In the image of the Image': Gregory of Nyssa's Opposition to Slavery	Adam Couchman (2023)
FP203	Gregory of Nyssa and the Sins of Asia Minor	Jonathan Farrugia (2023)
FP204	Discovery	Arthur Bell (2023)
FP205	Living Healing: the Spirituality of Leanne Payne	Andy Lord (2023)
FP206	Still Listening: Sowing the Seeds of the Jesus Prayer	Bruce Batstone CJN (2023)
FP207	Julian of Norwich: Four Essays to Commemorate 650 Years of the Revelations of Divine Love Bishop Graham Usher, Father Colin CSWG, Sister Elizabeth Ruth Obbard OC, Mother Hilary Crupi OJN (2023)	
FP208	TIME	Dumitru Stăniloae, Kallistos Ware (2023)
FP209	Pearls of Life: A Lifebelt for the Spirit	Tony Dickinson (2024)
FP210	The Way and the Truth and the Life: An Exploration by a Follower of the Way	James Ramsay (2024)
FP211	Cosmos, Crisis & Christ: Essays of Wendy Robinson	Wendy Robinson (2024)
FP212	Towards a Theology of Psychotherapy: The Spirituality of Wendy Robinson	Andrew Louth (2024)
FP213	Immersed in God and the World: Living Priestly Ministry	Andy Lord (2024)
FP214	The Road to Emmaus: A Sculptor's Journey through Time	Rodney Munday (2024)
FP215	Prayer Too Deep for Words	Sister Edmée SLG (2024)
FP216	The Prayers of St Isaac of Nineveh	Sebastian Brock (2024)
FP217	Two Medieval English Saints: Cuthbert and Alban	Sister Benedicta Ward SLG (2024)
FP218	Encountering the Depths	Mother Mary Clare SLG (1981, rev. 3/2024)
FP219	Conflict and Concord Sister Susan SLG, Bishop Humphrey Southern, Bronwen Neil, Sister Rosemary SLG, Sister Clare-Louise SLG (2024)	
FP220	Divine Love in the Song of Songs	Sister Edmée SLG (2024)
FP221	Zeal for the Faith: An Introduction to Christian-Muslim Dialogue	Tony Dickinson (2024)
FP222	Bernard & Abelard	Sister Edmée SLG (2024)
FP223	Eliot's Transitions: T. S. Eliot's Search for Identity and the Society of the Sacred Mission at Kelham Hall	Vincent Strudwick (2024)
FP224	Landscape, Soul and Spirit: Ecology, Prayer and Robert Macfarlane	Andy Lord (2025)

Contemplative Poetry Series

CP1	*Amado Nervo: Poems of Faith and Doubt*	trans. John Gallas (2021)
CP2	*Anglo-Saxon Poets: The High Roof of Heaven*	trans. John Gallas (2021)
CP3	*Middle English Poets: Where Grace Grows Ever Green*	ed. John Gallas (2021)
CP4	*Selected Poems: The Voice inside Our Home*	Edward Clarke (2022)
CP5	*Women & God: Drops in the Sea of Time*	trans. and ed. John Gallas (2022)
CP6	*Gabrielle de Coignard & Vittoria Colonna: Fly Not Too High*	trans. John Gallas (2022)
CP7	*Selected Poems: Chancing on Sanctity*	James Ramsay (2022)
CP8	*Gabriela Mistral: This Far Place*	trans. John Gallas (2023)
CP9	*Henry Vaughan & George Herbert: Divine Themes and Celestial Praise*	ed. Edward Clarke (2023)
CP10	*Love Will Come with Fire*	Sisters of the Love of God (2023)
CP11	*Touchpapers*	coll. and trans. John Gallas (2023)
CP12	*Seasons of my Soul*	Clare McKerron (2023)
CP13	*Reinhard Sorge: Take Flight to God*	trans. John Gallas (2024)
CP14	*Embertide: Encountering Saint Frideswide*	Romola Parish (2024)
CP15	*Thomas Campion: Made All of Light*	ed. and introd. Julia Craig-McFeely (2024)

Vestry Guides

VG1	*The Visiting Minister: How to Welcome Visiting Clergy to Your Church*	Paul Monk (2021)
VG2	*Help! No Minister! or Please Take the Service*	Paul Monk (2022)
VG3	*The Liturgy of the Eucharist: An Introductory Guide*	Paul Monk (2024)

www.slgpress.co.uk

The Sisters of the Love of God is an Anglican community of women religious living a contemplative monastic life.

To learn more about the Community and the Convent of the Incarnation at Fairacres, Oxford, see our website www.slg.org.uk.

As well as supporting those seeking to follow a vocation to the monastic life, the Community has a number of forms of association for those who feel drawn to share in the Sisters' life of prayer: Fellowship of the Love of God, Companions, Priests Associate or Oblate Sisters.

For more information email sisters@slg.org.uk or write to The Reverend Mother, Convent of the Incarnation, Parker Street, Oxford, OX4 1TB, UK.